A GIFT FOR YOUR JOURNEY

TO LOVING YOURSELF

A gift for Your Journey to Loving Yourself

BY LINDA STRAIT

A Gift For Your Journey to Loving Yourself
© 2021 by Linda Strait

All rights reserved. No part of this book may be used or reproduced in any manner whatsoever, including internet usage, without written permission from Linda Strait, except in the case of brief quotations embodied in critical articles and reviews.

For ordering information, contact the author at www.lindastrait.com.

ISBN: 978-1-953596-13-0 (hardback)
ISBN: 978-1-953596-14-7 (paperback)
ISBN: 978-1-953596-15-4 (ebook)

Library of Congress Number:
2 0 2 1 9 0 5 5 4 4

First Edition, 2021
The Publishing Portal
www.thepublishingportal.com

Printed in the United States of America

OTHER BOOKS BY LINDA

A Gift for Your Journey: A Book About Loss and Greater Gain

DEDICATION

I dedicate this book to my teachers, my helpers, my guides, my friends. You are many and in many different forms. You have pushed me and held my hand. You have knocked me down and picked me up. You have turned me away and embraced me with open arms. Thank you.

PREFACE

My journey to finding what was missing in my life—feeling connected, confident, peaceful and whole, came at a time when life had become stale and mundane. The last thing I wanted was to live a mundane life. I sensed a spirit, a stirring, within me that I had ignored for some time while I acquired the "stuff" that society approved of. It didn't make me happy. Having others' approval was losing its allure. I would rather be happy than approved of. I wanted to be authentic.

I'm sharing my journey with you, and I'm betting that you can identify with it. As it turns out, when we individually identify our truths, we are led to accepting, trusting and loving ourselves. That brings us to the connective love between us that we have each been seeking.

I can feel you and your big heart, and it makes me smile. I know that we are connected in a way that is strong, permanent and true. I embrace you as my tribe. I am grateful for you. Happy Journey!

Love,
Linda

What Can I Say?

What can I say
that will bring you to loving yourself fully?
What words will touch your heart
and make it sing with the knowledge of your greatness?
Deep within you, there is a seed
waiting to be born into the light of your light.
Coax it forth.
Nurture it as only you know how.
Let's watch it bloom together.

My Truth

There is no doubt when speaking my truth.
It has been uncovered and evolved
from the time after time of questioning it deeply.
Is this true for me---or false?
A-Ha moment after A-Ha moment has been revealed
allowing me to choose differently to establish a new truth;
allowing me to forgive myself each step of the way.
It is the <u>most</u> important journey I've ever taken,
filled with unknown freedom and unexpected insights
to bring me here, now.
A place that is grander than imagined.
A place where I can love freely
because I am freely loved—by me.
I give that gift to myself
and it overflows to you.

Serendipity

Serendipity is not magic, or chance.
It is God communicating
and me listening.

Open Your Heart

Practice opening your heart.
It's where all truth lies.
Not in your mind.
Not in your body.
Their source is your heart.
Acknowledge it---get to know it.
Let your highest self direct it,
until all of you becomes your highest self.

Choices

Is it—
Or is it not?
Yes or No?
Right or Wrong?
Good or Bad?
Love or Fear?
What a complex maze life is
until you learn to love yourself.

I AM More

I AM more
than I have allowed myself to own.
When I was surrounded by my shadows,
this "more" was scary.
My ego, in trying to keep me safe,
did not want me to venture forth to explore
what was beyond my human perception.
I had to fight for my freedom.
I was my opponent;
not others, not circumstances.
They were there to help me come to the point
of confronting my ego.
Keep climbing the mountain—
one foot in front of the other.
The peak has views that will free you,
and your heart will swell with the joy
of accomplishment.

Honoring Yourself

What can I say
that will touch your heart is such a way,
that you will never, ever, do that again?
Never forsake yourself;
Never give up on your deepest desire;
Never quit honoring your voice.
Your worth will not be revealed
on someone else's coattails.
Your worth is stand alone, power ranger strong.
Rooted in rightness,
All that IS.
Rise up and claim your heritage.
Open your heart and see what comes out.
There is more than you can imagine,
waiting for a chance to sing *your* song.
Allow, Allow, Allow

Isn't It Weird

Isn't it weird how just deciding to be happy
is so hard?
You would think it would be so easy—
What is there to think about? Just do it!
Well, there's the dwindling bank account,
the extra pounds, the car repairs,
the petulant child
all calling you to sink to their level
of awareness.
This 3rd dimensional world is a drag—
Literally.

I'm Waiting

When will it happen?
That thing that I'm waiting for—
that lets me know I've arrived.
To be sure, I have arrived at many places
but not *the* place.
The one that I've been striving towards my whole life.
Aware or not aware
Slowly—or with lightning speed
it still eludes me
I know—I'm told—it's a place within,
when you finally, fully, love yourself.
You will love where you are, who you are,
in each moment.
And I do…but still,
I know there is more
and it dangles before me like an elusive carrot.
When will it be *my* turn?
Oops—is that the victim in me standing in my path?
Dang!
Well, at least I recognize her.
More work to do—more weeds to pull

Rainbows

I see the end of the rainbow,
with all of its beauty and promises.
It is so close. So close.
I should reach it by night fall.
But my dogged pursuit,
keeps me from seeing the rainbow
that surrounds me.

Purging

I feel the urge to get it out:
To Purge!
To Spew!
To cleanse to my toes
and see what's left!
There is a lot left.
That I know.
I've built a foundation that is both
human and spiritual.
I've done it the hard way through my human experiences
but also the easy way, with many helpers.
So many helpers, standing by while I found my truth.
How could they love me that much,
when I haven't even loved myself?
It must be a spiritual thing—
not so much human.
So that's it—the goal—
To create human/spiritual assimilation.
I have faith that I love that <u>BIG</u>
without walls
unable to be anything else but love.
Love BIG
And that's all I need to do.

Human and Spiritual

How do I be human as a spiritual being?
I recognize fear and I do not choose it.
But where is the line
between human common sense and fear?
If I practice healthy eating
do I need vitamins?
If my Vibrational being is elevated,
do I need vaccinations?
Why can I not rise above these earthly experiences?
Because I am human.
And what exactly does being human mean?
That my choices have to be made every second
of every minute.
I must be diligent in my discipline.
It is one of the great lessons of human life.
Once I became aware and no longer live in a fog
Over, and over, and over I must ask myself:
Is this fear or love?
Then choose.

Awakening

I am awakening to my power.
The truth of it comes slowly to my human mind
It is paced by my willingness to allow it.
My ego still wants someone else to save me,
to shelter me,
to wrap me in strong arms and keep me safe.
But I have learned—
My ego only know a part of me-
the scared me.
My soul is my "go to"
and my ego follows
and together, as one,
we expand and soar.

How Do You Know?

How do you know when enough is enough?
When your soul tells you so.
Not your mind…
Not your ego.
Your soul.
The part of you where your wisdom sits and knows without a doubt
The part of you that stands up—
Consequences be damned!—
And says "ENOUGH"!

I Trust

I trust…
I trust…
kind of.
Why would I hold on to ego control?
It is not my friend…
It just <u>thinks</u> it is.
Tenacious as a narcissist at a debate tournament,
standing in my way to freedom.
I cannot fight it---
It takes too much energy.
Best to walk away and change paths.
I will look to the light
Follow the light,
Ahh… that's better!
I'm done with fighting my ego.

Signals

My body often signals me
that there is an emotion inside waiting to be heard.
My internal GPS that never fails to bring me closer to home.
I pay attention.
Get quiet…
and then invite the "me" that wants to be heard to come forward.
I listen intently
and say "tell me more"
Until I know that I've reached *The Point*
of what needs to be addressed.
And I speak to that hurt me who is looking for compassion and love,
and I give her exactly what she needs.
Because I love her so.
And now we can go forward
assimilated, in sync,
In Love
As ONE

Owning Your Shadows

Gut wrenching stuff.
Seeing the hurt that you caused and not backing down.
I did that.
I said that.
No excuses.
It clutches your heart—
brings tears to your eyes
and opens the doors wide to compassion
and Love
for Yourself.
I did that.
I am so sorry.

Rest When You Need To

Rest when you need to.
Choose to honor your body.
It is full of information that it wants to share with you.
Your life story,
packaged in skin and bones,
muscles and organs.
All systems firing
or not.
Hear their story.
Acknowledge their wisdom.

Have—Have Not

Where is my focus?
For the world is vast,
and both lists can be long.
What makes me feel empowered and happy?
That's what I want.
Empowered and happy is worth fighting for.
It's worth the unpleasant "tough love" for my ego.
Keep the focus on HAVE;
It's an ongoing campaign for my soul.
My HAVE muscle is getting stronger,
as I exercise it more.

Above All Else

Above all else,
I want to understand.
When I listen, see, experience,
with an open heart,
Understanding washes over me
and I am transformed
from someone who judges,
into a vessel for love.

Releasing to Enlightenment

How can one body hold so much?
Lies, deceit, protections
through eons and lifetimes,
until the burden becomes too great.
The releasing is painful as truths are exposed.
The enlightenment is…light…
the reward that makes it all worth it.
My ego feels awkward
not knowing how to be in this new me.
But my soul is there to comfort it
and say:
"There, there. It will be alright"
And life, my life, expands
and recognizes that it's always been alright.

Starting Again

Raw. Exposed.
No hiding here.
Out in the open for all to see.
Me. Reborn.
Starting at the beginning again
with Wisdom.

Training Ground

Here we are, together in a confusing world
As if an enormous hurricane came through
and left us alive, but shaken.
Everything we knew before is gone.
There are no landmarks,
No street signs.
Only destruction.
We have to rebuild.
We have to <u>Choose</u> how to rebuild
We begin as if an a dream
Guided by our instincts.
Blind
Numb
Not even knowing how to let the light in.
This is forced letting go.
This is choice when we didn't choose.
This is life lived behind veils and masks,
ignored until they were ripped off.
Can whole communities have called this to them?
That answer seems too easy.
True answers are simple, but not easy.
So what is true?
Not knowing, except through faith.
Having faith that the Big Picture is always for the greater good

Getting Your Attention

Pain gets your attention
like nothing else can.
When in pain, you finally stop ignoring...
Instead of pushing back, pushing down, you pay attention.
Somewhere in your unaware past,
you have asked for this.
It is a part of your journey planned by you,
at a time when you knew clearly
what you wanted to clear.
Give it your full attention.
Include your higher self in the listening.
Act with deliberation to free yourself.

Cracking Open—Or Cracking Up?

Which will you choose?
You are more powerful than you know,
and the choice is yours.
Will you look with eyes wide open,
or will you hide your eyes and refuse to see?
We all have shadows.
You are not better or worse than anyone.
We are all on the road to finding our magnificence.
Facing our shadows is a necessary part of the discovery.

Disbelief

Disbelief in myself
keeps me small.
I see myself as strong—
but powerful?
There is doubt.
God held nothing back in my creation.
I'm the one who brought disbelief into my cells.
I'm the one who must remove it.
And I want to…
but how?
I can ask for help—
I'm not alone—I have support…
But this is my job to do.

What is the fear that I'm required to surrender
in order to achieve full belief in myself?
It's lodged in my jaw, as if I were gripping for a reckoning
"Others—but not you."
"You are not yet ready"
Who's saying that?
Who's judging me?
At one time—eons ago—I chose to believe you.
Not now! I have gained wisdom.
So, Not Now! Not So! No!
I am ready
I accept.
I believe.

Splinters In My Heart

Thoughts,
Like splinters in my heart,
Hold me back from MYSELF
Why would I do that?
It's not what I choose or have to live with,
now that I am awake and aware.
A tiny sliver embedded where it does not belong
causes so much pain.
My heart wants the healing process to begin.
With pinpoint precision I dislodge the sliver
and hold it up to the light.
It looks harmless—but it's not.
It's what stood between me and joyful existence,
peaceful acceptance,
Sending it on its way—
transmuting its energy to love,
my heart begins to heal.

Tired and Despairing

Sometimes when I feel despairing
and tired and defeated,
I find within those feelings the most powerful lessons
and come to understand
that God's love is working within me.

Illusions

Surrounded by Love,
Inspiration,
Rightness…
and not being able to see it,
touch it,
smell it,
hear it,
know it
Is the deepest form of sadness.
It's only illusive
because of my illusions.
The ones that keep me stuck on my hamster wheel
in a space full of beauty beyond my wildest dreams.
I can't do this alone.
I need someone to help me slow this wheel,
so that I can step off.
Thank you!
You heard me!
You've been standing there all along—
just waiting for me to ask.

My Box

My very small, very limiting box
gave me a place to feel safe in my eerily quiet chaotic life,
while I was trying to figure everything out by myself.
Such a creative way
to stifle my creativity.
It was an illusion—
but it worked.
It was confining—
but it served me well.
It brought me to adulthood
where I could finally begin dismantling it.
Now I feel the possibility of what a creative life can be.
Did you know?
Creativity is another form of love.

Feeling Lost

Feeling lost---
but not really.
On the cusp of a "new me" expression,
without knowing what that is.
How do I speak? Process? Dress?
I haven't fully owned this new me.
She is still a mystery to me
and she makes me a bit uncomfortable.

Soft Spots

There are soft spots within me
that formed in my innocence,
when I believed everything that others said.
They were often wrong—for me.
My journey has been mining *my* truths,
the things that make me unique;
truths that no one else can decide for me.
I took their judgments into my beliefs blindly
but now, with awareness, I choose not to believe.
I decide my own truths.

Seeing the Light

Glaring in its brightness---
like a hood being ripped off after years of darkness
by someone outside of myself.
I could have taken it off earlier,
but I was "in the dark".
I didn't know what I couldn't see.
It brings a feeling of freedom.
Finally, understanding that I don't have to stay here
in the dark.
I don't have to continue to "do my duty"
long after it was no longer necessary.
My responsibility has been fulfilled.
I can walk away.
Now that I can see the light,
there are *many* adventures, *many* paths,
that I can choose.
It feels **joyful**.

I AM Love

I AM Love

In spite of the many human experiences that have told me—no—

You are not.

I AM Love

Innately…I can be nothing else.

But uncovering that truth from its deeply buried tomb

is the hardest thing I've ever done.

My eyes tear easily from the grief of life unlived,

because I accepted false truths without question.

I will rest a while in this sadness…

waiting for it to clear,

before I move into the new beginning that is sure to follow.

I will never turn back.

I will not be diverted.

I will embrace my light.

I AM Love.

Patience

Patience is so hard to come by…
once I finally know where I want to go,
Time, experience, my physical body,
move like molasses being sipped through a straw.
It will happen in its own time,
Completely absent of the knowledge of *my* timeline,
but fully aware of my state of mind.

Grounding vs. Grounded

I chose to be grounded
so I got to work grounding.
My foundation was weak
and grounding was challenging.
I uncovered false beliefs, discarded them
and arrived at my truths as I put down roots.
Being grounded is powerful,
Like a hurricane proof building.
I can now reach to the sky
feeling safe and expansive
regardless of what is swirling around me.

A-HA

Middle of the night A-Ha's
have become a way of life for me.
My soul likes to play at 3A.M.
She nudges me awake with her insight.
She has been waiting all day
for this invitation to come out to play.
I come, fully attentive,
Knowing that I will be so glad that I did.

Moments of Peace

There was a time
when moments of peace were enough—
but not now.
Now it is a state of being
that I want to live and breathe in forever.
To truly know that all is well in every moment.
No more tensing, clenching, holding of breath.
Instead, a beautiful easy flow
that creates and supports my vision of me
being Me.

Acceptance

Those who doubt us—
who don't believe in us…
have no room in our lives.
They are not ready to feel the greatness
that we have come to know
of God's expansive love for us.
They are not yet ready to receive our greatest gifts.

Families

And so it is that we are all family,
from the same source,
connected by love.
My family sustains me by challenging me—
motivating me to be different—
causing me to examine my most deeply buried false truths.
They push me toward establishing my own foundation
to speaking my own truth,
even though I am not understood.
Instead of being supported,
I am supporting.
Instead of being wrapped in unconditional love,
I am redefining what love is to me.
My family has taught me acceptance
of where my true power is…
and recognition of the Bigger Picture.
I get my unconditional love from a higher source
And all is well
I am Loved, I am Loving,
I AM LOVE

Feeling Safe

Feeling safe is exactly what I need
to feel free.
Without it—I brace myself, I live in fear,
always having that safety valve of "hiding" at my disposal.
Hiding my light—hiding me…
the ME that is a brilliant statement of God's love for me.
I am never *really* unsafe.
I live on and on and on, divinely protected
molded, formed by my choice to embrace or brace.
Today, I'm embracing.
Embrace---not brace
A world of difference.

Time to Move On

When you are not being heard—
when you've tried over and over to share your concerns
your deepest feelings
your longings—
only to be met with indifference,
it's time to move on.
Being ignored is a slow, painful death of a relationship.
It leaves you feeling empty inside,
with nowhere to turn—
except to turn away.
There is a new path waiting for your discovery.
One that supports you…
Believes in you…
Thinks you are amazing.
And that's all it takes to reignite your interest in life.
Because you see, you are just that—
AMAZING!
And your heart knows it.

No Failure

All is not lost.
There is no failure.
There *is* shift and adjustment
on your way to somewhere beautiful.

Love doesn't always look like love.
Sometimes it ROARS like anger;
Sometimes it comes as softly falling tears.
Sometimes it is so disguised
that you have to look deeply to see it.

Be at peace, even when you're not.
Hold on to the knowing
that everything is going to be OK.

There is goodness beneath the pain
There is kindness within the means
There is faith behind the doubt
There is hope within your heart

I Have Awareness

I do not fear
the attempts of others to manipulate me.
Whether or not they do it with awareness,
I have awareness
I am fine tuning my response
to move from reaction to choice.
It is a challenge that I relish.
It gives me power.

Dream Big

Sometimes I dream big
And when I do, I smile a lot.
It's my heart clapping for me
My soul doing a happy dance
My being…BEING

The Beauty of Relaxing

When I relax,
I let go of tension
in my jaw, shoulders, throat,
and I find a shift in attitude.
I recognize how little really matters.
The lists, the have-to's, are nothing
compared to the taking time to connect with myself.
I let go of feeling rushed—of needing to be somewhere else,
and open up to the beauty of me.
I realize, while warmth spreads from my heart,
just how much I love myself.

The Peace That Comes After The Storm

The peace that comes after the storm
is sweet in its harshness.
Scabs ripped off to reveal new life.
Life that doesn't "know" what can go wrong—
because nothing is wrong.
A fresh beginning and a deeper acceptance of what will come,
based on what I choose to allow.
I am at peace with this peace.
I'm in no hurry to leave this feeling of soft hope…
of tiptoeing through the unknown.
It's like a treasure hunt through my personal attic---
created just for me.
Beautiful things are stored here.
What will catch my eye?
I relish making the choice.
Life is deeply rewarding.

Today

I have this whole, beautiful day to myself
to do whatever I choose.
Will the deliciousness of that
keep me fed and nourished all day?
Or will I sink into chaotic thinking again?
Probably, but oh well,
I know how to remove myself from that.
It takes practice
to be practically perfect
It takes letting go
to BE in perfection.

Winter Growth

Even in winter there is growth.
It springs forward
from deep rest.
It subtly tickles the back of your throat
and finds its way to form the air
behind your words.
Do not dismiss the importance of this.
It's life changing stuff.

Another Chance

Like Noah and the flood
we are getting another chance,
while living with our chances by unconscious choice.
Pay attention this time.
Be very aware of your choices—
and know that maybe…
you are ready for something BIG

New Day

This is a new day
like all of the others, only different
because this is my current new day.
My heart feels hopeful
My mind is peaceful
In spite of all that is swirling around me
I choose to invest my attention
in my own glorious story.

Permission To Play

I used to feel guilty—
so much work to do!
But now it dawns on me—
this adult needs to play!
Play Big. Play Hard. Use my energy for Fun.
That's how I'll save the world!
Passing from one overworked, trying to be perfect human, to another
the remembrance of play.
When you play,
you are not angry
or fearful
or worried.
You just play.
That is living in the moment.
A perpetual God-given gift.
A statement of pure, deep faith
that really and truly
All is Well.

Your Story

From my heart to yours
I want you to know
that so much doesn't matter.
It doesn't matter—your story,
because in the end,
after you've wound your way through the maze,
it's just a story.
A story created to bring you full circle
to who you really are:
Magnificent.
Grander than Grand.
Humble, Beautiful, Perfect…
in the eyes of your creator.
Now you can let go of the story.
Stand strong and steadfast in the truth:
You Are Enough
You Have Enough
All Is Well.

Days In The Sun

What's coming up for examination?
What's being asked if it's true?
Old habits under the microscope;
attitudes that don't serve the new, awakened me.
Any quick responses, I choose to examine carefully.
I want no extra baggage.
My movements have become strides,
arms swinging freely,
body no longer creaky and painful.
Welcome Life!
Welcome Love!
I have prepared for you
and my Days In The Sun.

Free At Last

Free at last
To recognize **Love**
See it, feel it, touch it, smell it;
take it in with each breath that I take.
This is the belonging that I craved.
This is the connection that I no longer *long* for---
because I have it.
It truly is all around me—
in the smallest particle of my individual cells…
in the atmosphere that surrounds me, like a vast ocean stretching
to eternity.
Such a feeling of calm…peace…washes over me.
It allows me to let go of the tension that I have been carrying for
decades.
Will my body know how to move—
now that I have removed my restrictive fences?
I'm in the process of finding out.
This is an adventure that is changing my life.
I move forward with a calm, curious, passion to experience my day
and the *rest of my life*.

True Love

When you <u>know</u>
that everything is from the same source—
which is true Love,
your eyes are opened to see in a different way.
The hurt, the anger, the deep wounds
are rooted in Love.
You have to experience what can crack you open
to reveal what's inside.
And it's Love—
Always Love—
In your face, soft, Love.
As your Love expands--released from its' hiding place—
life makes sense.
You accept the awesome greatness of the universe
and you trust.
You TRUST.

A Knowing

There is a knowing that comes to you---
like experiencing the <u>most</u> beautiful dawning,
that all along---*all along*—you have been loved and cared for.
Your story is just that---a story.
When you have done the work of uncovering the deeply buried
parts of your story,
and you can look at it with your new perspective,
You <u>*know!*</u>
You know Love.
It permeates you, surrounds you, and carries you forward like a
magic carpet.
Only it's real.
The most real thing you've ever experienced as a human.
Take up your walking stick and put one foot in front of the other.
stop to rest, but do not <u>*stop.*</u>
You will be rewarded with the wisdom, the knowledge, the
understanding,
of who you <u>**really**</u> are
and it is magnificent.
I love you, truly.

My Place in the Ocean

My place in the ocean is my place alone.
No one—No thing—occupies my space except ME.
The ME that has formed through lifetimes of unique experiences
of mine alone.
It is my contribution to the whole.
No more, no less, than anyone else's—
and that is the beauty of it.
The "different, but equal" of it.
Together we are the pulse of the Universe
We *are* the Universe.
Infinite Ones being
ONE

Keep Your Eye on the Prize

There will be many times
when you consider stopping.
"I've done enough."…
"It's too hard"…
"I can't"
Don't allow those thoughts to take root in your cells.
You have the light within you
that contains everything you need to succeed.
GOD I AM SUCCESS
Say it over and over and over
and watch it become true.

The Best of Me

From a place of strength,
I choose.
From a place of peace,
I choose.
From a place of Love,
I choose.
My choices cannot be toppled,
for they come from the very best of me,
the connected me,
my highest self.
I walk in the world with grace
and all is well.

ABOUT THE AUTHOR

Linda lives in Springfield, Missouri where she works, plays with friends and family, and plans her next trip.

Her business career was in the travel industry—a family owned travel agency that evolved, until the changing times of technology helped her to decide to sell. She enjoyed the challenge of owning a business, until it became too challenging to be fun anymore. A different motivation took over as the quest for joy demanded her attention.

She began to actively seek knowledge and wisdom that would give a deeper satisfaction with life. She studied and practiced Reiki, Qigong, Past Life Therapy and Yoga, and attended workshops of authors that resonated with her. As she sorted through the new perspectives she was acquiring, the A-Ha moments, she began to journal.

Life experiences have taught her the power of words—both the damage and the healing that they can do. She loves the medium of poetry because it is a concise, powerful way to transmit feelings and thoughts. This is her calling, to use her words to lift others up and help them find their own joy. Although expressing what is in her heart through poetry has come later in life, the profound truths that she expresses have come from a lifetime of experiences.

Linda is available for custom poems that are perfect for gifting others or yourself. For more information, visit her website at www.lindastrait.com.

www.ingramcontent.com/pod-product-compliance
Lightning Source LLC
Chambersburg PA
CBHW071423070526
44578CB00003B/667